First published in Great Britain in 2015 by Osprey Publishing

PO Box 883, Oxford, OX1 9PL, UK

PO Box 3985, New York, NY 10185-3985, USA

E-mail: info@ospreypublishing.com

Osprey Publishing is part of Bloomsbury Publishing PLC

© 2015 Alex Fleetwood and Osprey Publishing Ltd.

All rights reserved. Apart from any fair dealing for the purpose of private study, research, criticism or review, as permitted under the Copyright, Designs and Patents Act, 1988, no part of this publication may be reproduced, stored in a retrieval system, or transmitted in any form or by any means, electronic, electrical, chemical, mechanical, optical, photocopying, recording or otherwise, without the prior written permission of the copyright owner. Enquiries should be addressed to the Publishers.

A CIP catalogue record for this book is available from the British Library

Print ISBN: 9781472813954
PDF e-book ISBN: 9781472815064
EPUB e-book ISBN: 9781472815071

Typeset in Officina Sans and Franklin Gothic
Originated by PDQ Media, Bungay, UK
Printed in China through Woldprint Ltd.

15 16 17 18 19   10 9 8 7 6 5 4 3 2 1

www.ospreygames.co.uk

Osprey Publishing supports the Woodland Trust, the UK's leading woodland conservation charity. Between 2014 and 2018 our donations will be spent on their Centenary Woods project in the UK.

TINY GAMES FOR WORK

BY

Hide&Seek
Inventing new kinds of play

ILLUSTRATED BY
PAULINA GANUCHEAU

HELLO!

THIS BOOK IS NOT DESIGNED TO BE READ IN ORDER.

Skip this introduction and open any random page to get playing. Alternatively, head to the back of the book for games suggestions and a full listing of games by number of players.

INTRODUCTION

GAMES ARE JUST AS POPULAR NOW AS THEY HAVE BEEN FOR THOUSANDS OF YEARS.

It's sometimes tempting to think of them as a newer cultural phenomenon, but we've had some form of them throughout all of recorded history. What *has* changed is the scale.

When I think about games now, I think about the biggest football matches, the most engrossingly huge videogames. Everything is epic in scale, it's like all stories have defaulted to being *War & Peace*.

When I think of some of my most happy memories of games, I think of my childhood. Playing cards at Christmas, standing on the sofa because a Micro Machines race is so tense, inventing a game with a ball, and a bat, and a see-saw in the green behind our house. These games were not more special because of some magical childhood perspective. They were more special because I had the time to dedicate myself to play.

In an era where so much focus is put on how hard we work, and how hard we play, it's worth remembering two key things: harder is not always better, and work and play are not opposites.

So, because time is at a premium, here is a book full of tiny ways you can bring play back into your working day. Some of them may be too silly for your tastes, or too awkward (or too conspicuous!) but all of them will be fun. Think of this book as a way to keep the days which drag on entertaining, and a way to give the days which fly by more weight. Use it to remember that play can be soft, and quick, and sneaky. Allow yourself time to dedicate to play, because the time it needs is tiny.

Have fun!

– Duncan Molloy, Osprey Games

DESERT ISLAND THINGS

A GAME FOR SURVIVALISTS AND THEIR STUFF.

In this game you're going to gather objects from around you which would help you survive on a desert island. You'll have thirty seconds to gather five things – the best-prepared survivor wins.

Set a timer for 30 seconds (use your phone or an egg timer) and run! Once you've picked something up, don't put it down! If you do, your opponent can take it for themselves.

After 30 seconds whose pile is best? See if you can agree – if not, sadly you're too argumentative to survive a wreck together. Why not take your objects to a real desert island to test them?

AUTOCOMPLICATED

DO YOU HAVE A TELEPHONE WITH VOICE RECOGNITION FOR DICTATION?

To play, you'll write an email using the phone's dictation function. Create and address a new email. To a friend, perhaps, or – for an extra challenge – for work. Now dictate the email.

You CANNOT remove any words or mistakes it makes. However, you can add words anywhere in the email to help it all make sense... To win, send it. Never tell the recipient how you wrote it.

THANKS CLIVE

DO YOU HAVE A MEETING COMING UP? AND ARE YOU WILLING TO GET AWKWARD?

Using someone's name in a conversation supposedly strengthens the bond between you. But how often is too often? During your meeting, try to say the names of people around the table as much as possible. Award yourself one point each time you use someone's name. Keep your own tally of your score.

At the end of the meeting, compare scores to discover who won. Try playing again, this time only scoring points for using one colleague's name. It's bound to make them feel cherished.

SAFE SEARCH OFF

DO YOU HAVE ACCESS TO THE INTERNET?

Image search engines often throw up baffling results, so could you guess someone's search term if you only saw the picture results? The person who takes the most photos is the Searcher, and everyone else is a Guesser. Searcher, secretly choose one word and search for it on Google Images. Carefully covering up the address bar (so you don't give the game away), show the Guessers the first few images from your search results. Each Guesser now has one guess to figure out which word the Searcher looked up. They can't guess the same word as anyone else.

Searcher, reveal the word you searched for and judge which Guesser came closest. The winning Guesser becomes the new Searcher, looking up a word of their own. Continue until you're too puzzled or distressed by what you've found on the internet to go on. If you're truly bold, try again with Safe Search off.

PLEASE DON'T TOUCH THE ARTWORK

A GAME FOR TALKATIVE PLAYERS.

In this game you're going to talk about a secret object as if it's a work of art. It's up to the other players to figure out what you're talking about. Choose your first Curator to secretly pick an object somewhere in the room, and talk about it as though it were a work of art. Which artist created it? How? What does it mean?

Visitors can ask questions like 'Was the work from the artist's early or late period?' or 'What about the claims that it's a forgery?' Once you think you know what the artwork is, walk over and touch it. Curator: if someone touches the right object, call out 'Please don't touch the artwork!' Keep going till everyone's had a turn as Curator.

RED BOMBS

DO YOU WORK WITH EXPLOSIVE CUSTOMERS?

Normally you'd gladly help all customers, but right now any wearing red is a bomb. Selfishly pass them onto your colleagues to escape their blast and score points.

Decide together how long you'll play for: perhaps an hour, until your break, or until the end of your shift. Go about your working day like the professional you are, until you end up helping a customer wearing red. You've now got a bomb! Try to pass the customer onto another colleague to dodge the bomb.

Every time you do, score one point. However, if someone passes a bomb to you, you can't then pass it onto someone else. Once the time you agreed on is up, whoever has scored the most points wins. Why not decide on a different time slot?

CROSSED PATHS

IS THERE A WHITEBOARD NEARBY?

Drawing a line through a circle on a whiteboard is easy – until you're doing it with your eyes closed.

Whoever grabs a whiteboard marker first starts by drawing a big circle on the board. This is your playing space. Close your eyes, take a step forward, and draw a line through the circle.

Open your eyes and scribble out the smallest section of the split circle. This bit is gone. It doesn't exist anymore. Accept it and move on.

Up steps the next player, eyes closed, to try to draw a line through the remaining space. If you split it, scribble the smaller part out again. Take turns drawing lines and scribbling out. Anyone who fails to strike through the remaining space is knocked out.

Consider it a financial metaphor and declare this business training if you like.

PICKPOCKET

DO YOU HAVE A TABLE AND TWO COINS?

In this game the Guard will place two coins on a table, and keep watch. Vigilant. Stern. Unyielding. Meanwhile, the Pickpocket will try to snatch them away – without getting tagged by the Guard.

Take two coins, and place them on the table about shoulder-width apart. The sternest player starts as the Guard, and places their hands about a foot above the coins. Now the other player becomes the Pickpocket, and tries to snatch the coins... without letting the Guard touch their hands.

You get one point for every coin stolen – put them back in place after each theft. If you get caught, then swap roles. The first player to reach ten points wins.

POST-IT TOWERS

ARE THERE SOME POST-IT NOTES NEARBY?

In this game you'll have to build a tower out of post-it notes, then knock down the opposition! Everybody grab ten post-it notes and set a timer for three minutes. You have to create the tallest tower you can using only your post-it notes. But be frugal! If you have any left after the three minutes are up, you can throw them at opposing towers to try to knock them down.

Going round the table, take turns to throw a (folded, screwed-up, whatever) post-it at any tower of your choice. Once you've all run out of post-its, the tallest surviving tower wins!

ADVERTICLE

IS THERE A NEWSPAPER OR MAGAZINE NEARBY THAT YOU CAN TEAR A LITTLE BIT?

In this game you're going to tear holes in a magazine to reveal part of the page behind. The question: is it an article or an ad?

The person who read a newspaper most recently is the Editor, and begins. As the Editor, your job is to look through the paper or magazine and secretly choose a picture. Now, tear a hole in a page to reveal a little bit of that picture – around an inch square, ideally.

Challenge the other player: is it an ad, or an article? Reveal the picture, then do it again with four more pictures. How many did they get right? If you play again, get a new magazine and swap roles.

EAGLE EYE

DO YOU HAVE SOME SMALL THINGS? COINS, PENS, KETCHUP PACKETS?

In this game, you'll set out an array of strange objects – coins, salt, toothpicks, anything. A treasury of excitement! But then it's time to take the treasury away, one by one. Who has the best memory about what was there? If you spot something missing, you add it to your pile o' treasures.

The player who most likes things starts. They're the Treasurer. Everyone else has to look away, or close their eyes. Treasurer: you have to find 15 small objects. Arrange them on the table, and when you're done tell the other players they can open their eyes for ten seconds. Count down! After ten seconds they have to close their eyes again.

Now it gets tricky: it's time to remove one object and pocket it. Tell everyone to open their eyes again – can they spot what's missing? Give the object to whoever figures it out fastest – they put it in front of them. Now repeat! They close their eyes, you remove an object, they try to identify it. Keep going till you're down to five objects. Whoever has the most stuff in front of them wins! They should probably put everything back. It's not REAL treasure, you know.

GOLD MEDAL IN BIRTHDAY REMEMBERING

ARE SEVERAL CUSTOMERS AROUND AND ARE YOU WILLING TO TALK ABOUT THEM?

What talented customers you have! Who knew that chap over there won bronze in Olympic Beard Growing? Who even knew it was an Olympic sport? It wasn't, of course, until you made it up. You'll declare mystery customers to be competitors in unusual Olympic events, as clues for the other player to guess who you're talking about.

Whoever most recently competed in an event goes first. Secretly choose a customer you can see to make into an Olympic hero. Based on their appearance and behaviour, make up an event they could have competed in.

Announce the Olympian, being careful not to indicate who you're talking about. 'He won silver in Jam-making,' you may declare, for example. Based on this, the other players must figure out which customer you're talking about. Take turns creating and guessing Olympians until every customer's secret talent has been uncovered. There, you're the Silver Medallists in Team Games...

NOT APRIL FOOL'S

A GAME OF DEFINITELY NOT PRANKING ANYONE.

'Mmm this coffee is delicious! You should try it! Go on! Drink some! You'll love it!' you insist. Your colleague eyes you up suspiciously: what are you up to? Nothing. You're not pulling any pranks of any kind, but you want everyone to think you are. The more suspicious they are, the more you win.

Approach colleagues with perfectly harmless offers which just happen to make it seem like you're trying to prank them. Award yourself one point every time you think someone refuses your offer because you're up to something (which you're definitely not!). Why not try playing on April Fool's Day?

SMALL TALK

A GAME OF SMALL SENTENCES.

This game is simple. Its sentences are short. You'll talk to each other. You will use short sentences. The sentences can't be long. You'll choose a topic. You'll discuss that topic. Sentences with six words: bad. You will keep it very brief. If you don't, you'll lose.

You'll start this game by saying 'Fancy some small talk?' Everyone will then have a conversation – adding sentences in turn. However, if anyone says a sentence more than five words long, they're out! They're also out if they can't think of something to say, or they start a sentence and can't finish it. The last player left in wins.

TIP: The second sentence should propose a topic, like 'How about Star Trek captains?' or 'What was Wenger thinking?' Talk short.

TRIANGULATED

ARE SEVERAL CUSTOMERS AROUND?

You may be skilled at avoiding customers, but how precisely can you stay away from them? One of you will pick out two customers, and the other must become the third point in an equilateral triangle with them.

Whoever's wearing the pointiest shoes is now the Triangulator, and the other is our Chooser. The Chooser needs to pick two nearby customers, and point them out to the Triangulator. The Triangulator then needs to form an equilateral triangle with these two customers by standing an equal distance from both.

When these customers move, the Triangulator must move too to keep your growing, shrinking or shifting triangle intact. The game's over either when one of the customers leaves, or if you break your equilateral triangle.

Then swap roles: the Triangulator must pick two customers, and the former Chooser needs to form a triangle with them. For a co-operative version, form a square...

MILK, NO SUGAR

DO YOU HAVE TEA AND COFFEE-MAKING FACILITIES?

Do you ever offer to make tea and coffee for everyone out the goodness of your own heart? Now you can turn your kindness competitive. You'll try to make tea or coffee for as many people as possible, but can only offer once a day. When will your colleagues be at their thirstiest? And will you turn down a cuppa to help you win?

Only once today, you each can ask around if people fancy a tea or coffee. Make the drinks. Hand them round. At the end of the day, whoever made the most drinks for other people is the winner – the most considerate workmate! Well done.

(No, you can't make drinks without being asked.)

VERY IMPORTANT INBOX

A GAME OF SELF-CONTROL AND INBOXES.

In this game you'll try to avoid constantly checking and rechecking your email. Every time you check your inbox today, if you don't have any new emails you earn 1 point. At the end of the day, if you have fewer than 3 points, you win. Why not set yourself a prize for success, or better yet, a forfeit for failure? Trust us, your inbox will be just fine without you.

BUSINESS AND PLEASURE 1

ARE YOU WILLING TO WRITE THINGS YOU DON'T WANT ANYONE ELSE TO EVER SEE?

Business? A simple work email you must write to a colleague. Pleasure? An erotic novel starring that same workmate. You'll write both at once, switching between them every 30 seconds. One goes to the colleague, the other goes to a friend. You can remember which is which, right?

Start two new blank e-mails, addressing one to a colleague you need to contact for work reasons and the other to a friend. For your first sentence, simply write your professional e-mail to the colleague. I'm sure you do this often, as a capable professional.

For the next sentence switch to your other email, the one addressed to your friend. This is where you'll write erotica starring your colleague. With some salubrious smut spilled out, return to the professional email. Keep switching back and forth every sentence until your work email is finished, then send both.

If it is a particularly lengthy email try switching every paragraph, and if you are concerned about naughty work emails, try some exciting fan-fiction about your colleague instead. You can finish the erotica in your own time, of course.

STANDING ORDER ②

ARE YOU OK WITH A GAME THAT MIGHT INVOLVE A LITTLE BIT OF GOSSIP?

You've surely never done it before, but it's time to rank and order your colleagues. You decide: is it by how tall they are, how much they spend on lunch, or how loud they are? But keep it secret. Reveal the order of several colleagues in your ranking. The other player must guess what this is in order of.

Whoever's been with the company longest is the Ranker, the other player is the Guesser. Ranker, secretly pick a rule to order colleagues by, anything you like. Now go stand near each of those three colleagues in the order in which they'd place in this ranking. (If you don't quite dare, just write their names down...)

Guesser, observe carefully and try to figure out the rule they've been ordered by. Guess away! Ranker, if the Guesser gets stuck, keep adding new people in order until the rule is revealed.

Then swap roles: the Guesser becomes the Ranker to create a new order, and the old Ranker must guess at it. Of course, some of the rankings may be controversial...

THAT'S NOT A PALM TREE

DO YOU ALL HAVE FACEBOOK ACCOUNTS AND INTERNET ACCESS?

In this game, you're going to be given an object – a coffee-cup, say; a palm tree; a swimming pool. Then you're going to race to find a picture showing that object – in your friends' Facebook photos.

Everyone agree on a random object, like 'Swimming Pool' or 'Bookshelf'. Once you've all agreed, you can open Facebook and race to find that object in a picture. You can ONLY look at photos your friends have uploaded or been tagged in. So, who went on a holiday lately? Who posts pictures of their lunch? Start thinking...

One point to whoever finds the object first. Keep going through objects and looking for them until someone has three points. If you're regularly a winner, maybe you just have better friends!

SPIN ME RIGHT ROUND

DO YOU HAVE A CHAIR THAT CAN SPIN AROUND?

As people with spinny chairs, you've surely mastered spinning your chair hard. But have you practised spinning with precision?

Following the whims of another player you'll need to spin your chair round and round and round and come to a stop pointing in the direction they choose. Closest to the target wins.

Each player will sit down in a spinny chair, spin it hard, then try to stop, pointing in a target direction. Someone will decide the direction everyone is trying to aim for. Players must close their eyes while spinning, and need to spin round at least three times. Whoever finished pointing closest to the target direction wins. If it was too close to call, make the closest spinners go again. SPIN. SPIN. SPIN.

THE POWER OF POSITIVE LISTENING

ARE THERE CHATTY PEOPLE NEARBY?

In this game you'll sit perfectly calm and still, listening to the voices around you until they say some specific positive words. Then you can holler, and pump your fists in victory.

Close your eyes and be perfectly still and quiet, though do remember to breathe. Listen to the voices around you, dipping in and out of all the different conversations. When you clearly hear someone say 'Yes,' 'Thanks,' or 'Good' you win. However, you lose if you open your eyes or move. Other than breathing, that is. (Really do keep breathing!)

FOOTLOOSE

DO YOU HAVE AN OFFICE CHAIR WITH WHEELS? ARE YOU WILLING TO WOOSH AROUND ON IT?

In this game, you're going to guess how far you could get around the office on a wheeled office chair, in one minute, without touching the ground. Whoever reckons they can get furthest has to prove it.

Whoever has been working here longest: look around the office. From where you are, how far do you think you could get on a wheely chair in ONE minute, WITHOUT touching the ground? You can push off desks, grab hold of door frames, anything like that – but not touch the floor.

Now invite everyone else to say how far they think they could go. Who thinks they can go the furthest? They have to prove it, while the others set a timer. If they fail, the next person who thought they could go furthest gets a chance for glory.

SPEECHLESS

CAN YOU SERVE CUSTOMERS SILENTLY WITHOUT GETTING IN TROUBLE?

In this game, you're going to see how many customers you can serve without words, and without confusing anyone. From now on until you stop playing, you can't speak. You can gesture, make noises, say numbers – but no words. How many customers can you serve in a row before you need to speak? See if you can beat that next time.

SCREEN BURN

2+

DO YOU USE A SCREEN?
OF COURSE YOU DO. SILLY QUESTION REALLY.

In this game you'll take a break from looking at the screen. All of them. The game begins immediately after you're done reading these rules. During the game, if any players look at the screen of a digital device, they immediately lose. It doesn't matter if the device is turned on or not, you still can't look at it. Also, even just glancing at a screen out of the corner of your eye counts. The last player remaining wins. (But seriously, what if you just got a very important email?)

NO, YOU HANG UP!

1

DO YOU HAVE AN EXCESSIVE
FONDNESS FOR VIDEO CALLS?

This is a game about not hanging up first. You don't want to seem rude, do you? Of course not. So... don't hang up before they do. Hold on. Just a bit longer.

Enjoy your video call, like the consummate professional you are, but when it reaches its conclusion, simply don't hang up. That's all: just don't hang up. Hold on and make them do the hanging-up. It's not awkward, is it? If they hang up first, you win! Now, the real question is: how many calls can you win in a row? Just hope you don't call anyone who's also playing...

DANGEROUS WORDS

DO YOU ALL HAVE PHONES ON YOU?

You're going to write text messages on each other's phones, adding a couple of words each at a time – and then you'll see who's bravest when it comes to actually sending them. To start, everyone take out your phone, open a new text message, and type two words. Now pass your phone to the person on your left and take a phone from your right. Add two words to the phone you've received, and then pass that one on as well.

Keep going until the messages are 12-16 words long. Now take your phone back and take turns to read out the text that's been composed. When you read yours out, say who you'd be willing to send it to – a friend? A partner? A boss? Agree on whose nominated recipient is funniest. If it's you, and you send the text, you win! Otherwise, you lose and everyone else wins. Play again, and see how many friends you can lose!

PHOTOCOP

IS THERE A PHOTOCOPIER THAT YOU CAN USE?

Congratulations, you're now all Photocop Internal Affairs deputies. Here are your badges and photocopiers. Now get out there and collect evidence by photocopying one another's stuff.

You don't know what you're investigating, only that each others' possessions are evidence. Stealthily confiscate, photocopy, then return them. Decide together how long you want to play for: one day, a week perhaps, or even a month. To collect evidence, sneakily swipe something from another Photocop, photocopy it, then return it. Add the copy to your evidence folder.

If another Photocop catches you copying evidence, you're out: your personal investigation is over and you can't collect any more. At the end of the agreed investigation period, or once every Photocop has been busted, present your evidence.

Whichever Photocop has collected the most evidence wins. Get copying! Documents, wallets, mugs – it all counts.

WRONG STATEMENT

DO YOU HAVE ANY MEETINGS COMING UP?

Questions! You've got loads of them. Burning questions. So many that you'll try to go an entire meeting speaking only in questions, without making a single statement. The player who lasts the longest, without giving in to the urge to make a statement, wins.

For a harder game, ban gestures as well...

WHIPPERSNAPPER

A WORD GAME OF USING THE SAME LETTER MANY TIMES.

Find a random letter and think of words containing that letter as much as possible. The player whose name comes last alphabetically should go first. Someone else quickly shout out a random letter. The player has to think of a word which uses this letter a whole load of times. Tell your word to everyone, then start counting up to ten. They all then have ten seconds to think of a longer one.

Whoever comes up with the word which has that letter the highest number of times is the winner. If you can't define it, it doesn't count! Unless it's more fun the other way. The winner gets to pick the next word to beat.

SECOND HAND REMBRANDT

IS THERE A WHITEBOARD NEARBY?

This game is co-operative – you're working together to keep going as long as you can. One of you will draw a picture, then the others will keep changing it into something completely different, with an ever-decreasing number of lines.

The player with the artiest name begins. Draw a picture on the whiteboard. Maybe a hamburger, or a self-portrait, or some sunflowers? Up to you. Hand the pen to the next player. They have to turn the picture into something completely different! They can erase as many lines as they want, but can only add ten.

You want to make something completely different – but the others need to be able to guess what it is. Now hand the pen on again – this time, the artist can only add NINE lines. Keep going! Eight lines next time, then seven. The game's over when people can't guess what you've drawn. How few lines can you get down to?

FRIEND OR FOE

DO YOU SERVE CUSTOMERS?

In this game you'll have a secret Friend customer and a secret Enemy customer. Win by helping the right one! Pick two customers you can see, choosing one to be your friend and the other your foe.

If your friend approaches you and asks something, you score one point. But if your foe needs help, you'll lose one point. After helping either, you must pick two new customers. Maybe you'll be better at choosing your friends this time. Can you reach ten points by the end of your shift?

ACCENTED CLOTHING

DO YOU SERVE CUSTOMERS?
HAVE YOU GOT A LOVELY VOICE?

One lucky customer will be treated to a display of your mastery of accents, though hopefully they'll never realise it's an act.

Pick an item of clothing you're likely to see a customer wearing, like shorts, sunglasses, or a scarf. Now pick an accent, such as Canadian, Liverpudlian, or Australian. Whoever feels most confident in their mastery of accents will go first.

When a customer comes in wearing the chosen item, our talented actor must speak to them in that accent. If you can serve them without getting a funny look whenever you open your mouth, you've both proven your acting prowess and scored a point. If not, it's back to acting classes with you. Either way, the next player will have a go now.

Pick another item and a new accent, and wait for another customer to volunteer themself by walking in wearing that. Keep going with new items and accents until everyone has had three turns. Whoever has scored the most points is the winner! Why not try having every player use the same accent?

BUSINESS!

DO YOU HAVE A STACK OF OTHER PEOPLE'S BUSINESS CARDS?

You've pocketed every business card you've been slipped, thinking you may need them one day. That day has finally come! Let's play snap. Instead of matching numbers, you'll be looking out for matching fonts, colours, job titles, and so on. And, as professionals, rather than cry 'Snap!' you'll exclaim 'Business!'

The player who arrived at work earliest today deals the business cards out, face-down, between everyone. That player then turns over the top card of their stack and places it face-up in the middle of the table. The next player, moving clockwise, turns over their top card and places it on top of that. Watch keenly.

As play goes round and the center stack grows, players must watch for anything the same on the top two cards: fonts; colours; job titles; companies; and so on. If you spot a match, slap your hand down on the pile and cry 'Business!' to win all those cards. Add them to the bottom of your personal pile.

Keep going until only one player has any cards left: the winner! The winner, clearly, is also the most attentive and sincere networker.

2002 BERLIN THUNDER SEASON

DO YOU HAVE A COMPUTER WITH INTERNET ACCESS AND WORK E-MAILS TO SEND?

You are subject to the obscure facts of chance!

Go to Wikipedia and click on 'Random article'. Note and copy the full title of your fascinating factually-accurate* article. You must now subtly slip this full title somewhere into the next work e-mail you send.

Repeat until satisfied, or until questioned about your references to obscure byelaws and pop songs. If you want to keep score, count how many you can fit into a single e-mail...

*[citation needed]

PUNCHED WHOLE

DO YOU ALL HAVE A HOLE PUNCH?

In this game, you'll each have twenty seconds to punch as many holes in a piece of paper as you can. To begin, give everyone a hole punch and a piece of paper. Set a timer for twenty seconds: you have this time to punch as many holes as you can. The only rule is that if two holes join up, those only count as ONE hole – so be careful.

Count up all the holes! Who has the most? Give it another go and see if you can beat the record...

IN SHAPE

COMBINE YOUR TWIN LOVES OF RUNNING AND GEOMETRY.

From cars to chihuahuas, it seems almost everything is made of shapes nowadays. But do you have what it takes to spot them? Someone will name a random shape, which everyone will need to race around trying to spot and reach.

Shape-spotters, you're about to be told a shape to find. The first to spot and touch one wins. Another player picks a shape, but keeps it tricky! We suggest things like Crescent, Hexagon, Star, or even a Squiggly Line. Whoever raced to the most shapes wins, and picks the shapes the next time you play.

SPACE STEALERS

IS THERE SOME STUFF AROUND? FORKS, PENS, STAPLERS, NECKLACES, WHATEVER.

In this game, you're going to take turns to add objects to the playing space. But be careful: the objects can't touch each other, or go off the edge of the playing space.

First, choose a playing area – a small table, a big book, anything flat. Now, get a pile of stuff. Avoid tiny or huge things – medium-sized works best. Now, take turns to add one thing from the pile of stuff to the playing area.

If your object touches another object, or goes off the edge of the playing area, you're out. The last player remaining wins.

DEADLY ACQUAINTANCES

ARE YOU WILLING TO GOSSIP ABOUT MUTUAL FRIENDS?

Given his love for baking, it's no surprise that it was Peter who struck with poisoned pastries as The Sweet Tooth. But could you guess it was him if you only knew the nickname and murder method?

Whoever's most likely to already be a secret murderer goes first. It's time for you to turn a friend into a killer. Secretly pick a mutual acquaintance. Based on their interests and personality, decide their serial killer nickname and favoured method of murder. Tell their nickname and modus operandi to the other player. They must figure out which friend it is based on these alone. Once the case has been solved, the other player must see the worst in a friend and turn them into a killer for you to guess. If you play again, maybe try actors or writers instead of friends!

STOCK TAKE

REARRANGE YOUR WORKPLACE AS MUCH AS YOU DARE.

This plant? It'd look far better on the other side of the room. In fact, all of it would. Everything. Let's move it.

Whoever's seen as the most sensible goes first. Pick up a small item and move it to somewhere on the opposite side of the room. The next player must choose something larger and shift that to the other side. Then the next player, and the next. On you all go, bigger and bigger each time.

Run out of bigger objects? Too chicken to shift the photocopier, or unable to shunt a cash register? It's all over! Keep the increase in size gradual, if you can...

FOLK ETYMOLOGY

A GAME ABOUT WHERE WORDS COME FROM.

In this game, you're going to be given a word and then compete to come up with an explanation of where the word comes from. The fake explanations have to be acronyms – like how 'laser' stands for 'Light Amplification by Stimulated Emission of Radiation'.

Agree on a word you can see from where you're sitting. You're going to try to come up with an explanation of what the letters in that word stand for. So, 'cat' might stand for 'Creeping Animal

Type'. Or 'tea' might be 'tepid, edible, aromatic'. Once you've got an explanation, say 'ready'. When everyone's ready (or has given up), you'll recite your explanations. Agree on the best – if you can't agree, call a friend and get them to judge. Use the last word of that explanation as the new word. First to three is the winner!

SOUNDS LIKE QUITE A SHIRT

A GAME ABOUT BEING VERY NICE.

In this game you'll give customers a compliment, and be scored according to how impressive it is.

The next time you speak with a customer, compliment them on something they're wearing. You'll earn 1 point for every time you say the word 'very' within the compliment. For example, saying 'That's a very very nice hat.' would earn you 2 points. Saying 'Oh my, that's a very very very VERY VERY striking pair of sandals!' would earn you 5 points.

Be careful: if at any time the customer gives you a look as if to say 'Um leave me alone you weirdo' then you forfeit all points. Legend has it that the world record for this game is 114.

SIDE SWIPE

DO YOU HAVE ANY VIDEO CALLS COMING UP?

At the end of a long day, nothing beats a good lie-down! If a video call stands between you and that rest, well, they couldn't tell you were lying down, could they?

It's simple: rotate yourself and your computer or camera 90 degrees so you're on your side. Now enjoy a productive video call. If the person you're calling spots that you're on your side, you lose. And may have some explaining to do. Too easy? Try taking the video call upside-down.

SECRET SINGER

ARE YOU MUSICALLY INCLINED?

In this game everyone will work to secretly slip song titles into the conversation, without being too obvious about it. Each player secretly picks a musician or band (preferably one whose songs they know well). Now subtly fit song titles into your conversation. See how many you can slip through without being caught.

If you can figure out someone's secret choice of band, accuse them. If you're right, they're out of the game. The winner is the first person to get three song titles through.

SPIRALLING OUT 2+

IS THERE A WHITEBOARD NEARBY? AND ENOUGH MARKERS FOR EVERYONE?

In this game you're going to draw spirals around each other, without letting your lines cross or taking your pen off the board. The more you can fit on the whiteboard, the better your score.

You'll need to start by putting your pens in the middle of the whiteboard. Now, spiral outwards around each other. Your pens must not leave the board or change hands. Your lines must not leave the board or cross. So you're going to have to do a bit of ducking under each other's arms...

You get a point for each complete circuit you manage to fit in – how many can you squeeze in before you run out of space or cross lines? The more people you add, the harder it gets...

EYES DOWN

DO YOU HAVE ANY MEETINGS COMING UP?

Making eye contact is polite, but what if a game is at stake? In *Eyes Down* you'll try to make eye contact with one player as much as possible, while avoiding another. Each player scores points by catching the attention and eye of the player to their right. This means you're also politely ignoring whoever's to your left, or they'll score.

Before your meeting starts, work out who's playing. You may wish to use discretion in asking people to goof off. Any time a player makes eye contact with the player to their right during the meeting, they score one point. Discreetly keep your own score. After the meeting, reveal and compare your scores. Whoever has scored the most points wins. Feel free to use props (snacks? The water jug?)

PAPER CHASE

DO YOU HAVE MORE THAN ONE COPY OF THE SAME NEWSPAPER?

If you'd like to keep informed of goings-on in the world but simply don't have time to read the newspaper, crash through the day's news with this game. Make sure each player has a copy of the same issue of the same newspaper. Whoever most recently bought a newspaper goes first. Have a flick through the paper and secretly choose an article. Start reading the article out loud.

The other players must race to find the article you're reading. If a player finds the article while you're still reading, they win. If you finish reading it, you win. Take turns reading out and finding articles. Feeling better-informed about world affairs yet?

DON'T DRAW THE SHORT STRAW

DO YOU HAVE PENS AND PAPER, AND AN ODD NUMBER OF PLAYERS?

In this game you'll be drawing straws. On paper. With pens or pencils.

Give everyone a piece of paper and a pen. Everyone should secretly draw a straw. You want your straw to be the medium-sized straw. Once everyone has finished REVEAL YOUR STRAWS!

The people who drew the LONGEST and the SHORTEST straw are both out – the happy medium straw is what it's all about. Now, repeat until only one player remains. All the drawings of straws are theirs – a glorious prize!

ONE-LINER

DO YOU HAVE SOME PAPER AND A PEN AROUND?

In this game one of you – the Drawer – will try to make a drawing as complete as possible without giving away what it is. Another player – the Saboteur – will try to guess what it is, and ruin things for the Drawer.

The player whose name sounds most like 'Picasso' is the first Artist, and the player whose name sounds least like 'Picasso' is the first Saboteur. Artist: you're going to choose something to draw – but you don't want the Saboteur to guess what it is. If the Saboteur does guess, then your turn is over, and they get a point.

When you're almost done, call out 'almost done'. At this point, the Saboteur can no longer guess. You now have one second to draw one line (curvy or straight). Everyone else has one guess about what you drew. If they get it, you and they get a point. Keep going until everyone has had two turns as Artist and as Saboteur. The player with the most points wins.

YOU LOSE

DO YOU HAVE A SHARED PRINTER?

You can find all sorts of weird documents abandoned in the printer tray. Look at this, for example: a sheet of paper which simply says 'YOU LOSE.' Oh. You can guess what that means.

Print out a page blank except for the words 'You lose.' Style them as simply or as extravagantly as you please. Don't collect the page from the printer. Simply leave it there.

Whoever picks that sheet up first is the loser. You don't need to tell them: they already know. They'll appreciate your contribution.

LAST MAN STANDING

DO YOU HAVE ANY MEETINGS COMING UP?

Countless esoteric etiquette rules govern when to stand and sit down in meetings, but this game follows one simple rule: you sit, you lose.

Before your meeting, agree on who'll be playing. When you go in for the meeting, the last player to sit down wins. At the end of the meeting, why not play Last Man Sitting? You can figure out the rules.

18 HOLES

DO YOU HAVE A HOLE PUNCH HANDY?

In this game, you're going to punch holes through some sheets of paper, all higgledy-piggledy over the page. You'll all have an identical hole-covered sheet of paper. Your aim will be to draw a line through each hole – using as few straight lines as possible.

Make a stack of papers – with one piece for each player. Now punch holes all over the paper as randomly as you can, not just at the edge. Give each player a piece of paper, a pen, and a ruler or book. Players: try to draw a straight line through every single hole, using as FEW lines as you can. If you used the fewest lines, you win!

APPENDIX

NUMBER OF PLAYERS	1	2	3	4+	PAGE
18 Holes		•	•	•	42
2002 Berlin Thunder Season		•	•	•	30
Accented Clothing	•	•	•	•	27
Adverticle		•			8
Autocomplicated	•				1
Business and Pleasure	•				15
Business!		•	•	•	28
Crossed Paths		•	•		5
Dangerous Words			•	•	22
Deadly Acquaintances		•			32
Desert Island Things		•	•	•	1
Don't Draw The Short Straw			•	•	39
Eagle Eye			•	•	9
Eyes Down			•	•	37
Folk Etymology		•	•	•	33
Footloose		•		•	20
Friend or Foe	•				26
Gold Medal in Birthday Remembering		•	•	•	10
In Shape			•	•	31
Last Man Standing		•	•	•	42
Milk, no sugar		•	•	•	13
No, you hang up!	•				21
Not April Fool's	•				11
One-Liner			•	•	39
Paper Chase		•	•	•	38
Photocop			•	•	23

NUMBER OF PLAYERS	1	2	3	4+	PAGE
Pickpocket		•			6
Please Don't Touch the Artwork		•	•	•	4
Post-It Towers		•	•	•	8
Punched Whole		•	•	•	30
Red Bombs		•	•	•	5
Safe Search Off			•	•	3
Screen Burn		•	•	•	21
Second Hand Rembrant			•	•	25
Secret Singer		•	•	•	35
Side Swipe	•				35
Small Talk		•	•	•	11
Sounds like quite a shirt	•				34
Space Stealers		•	•	•	31
Speechless	•				20
Spin Me Right Round		•	•	•	17
Spiralling Out			•	•	37
Standing Order		•			16
Stock Take			•	•	33
Thanks Clive		•	•	•	3
That's not a Palm Tree			•	•	17
The Power of Positive Listening	•				18
Triangulated		•			12
Very Important Inbox	•				13
Whippersnapper			•	•	25
Wrong Statement		•	•	•	23
You Lose		•	•	•	40

TINY TIPS

IMPORTANT MEETING COMING UP?

- Show your attentiveness with **Thanks Clive** — 3
- Interrogate your co-workers **Wrong Statement** — 23
- Keep your **Eyes Down** — 37
- Try to be the **Last Man Standing** — 42

SERVING CUSTOMERS?

- Avoid those **Red Bombs** — 5
- Keep your customers **Triangulated** — 12
- Complement what **Sounds Like Quite a Shirt** — 34
- Try for a **Gold Medal in Birthday Remembering** — 10

STUCK AT YOUR DESK?

- Race through your friends with **That's Not a Palm Tree** — 17
- Share your desk with some **Space Stealers** — 31
- Combine some **Business AND Pleasure** — 15
- Rest your eyes from **Screen Burn** — 21

FEELING COMPETITIVE?

- Dust off your detective skills with **Photocop** — 23
- Celebrate mediocrity with **Don't Draw the Short Straw** — 39
- Keep fit with **In Shape** — 31
- Get organised with a **Stock Take** — 33